MW01627359

Welcome!

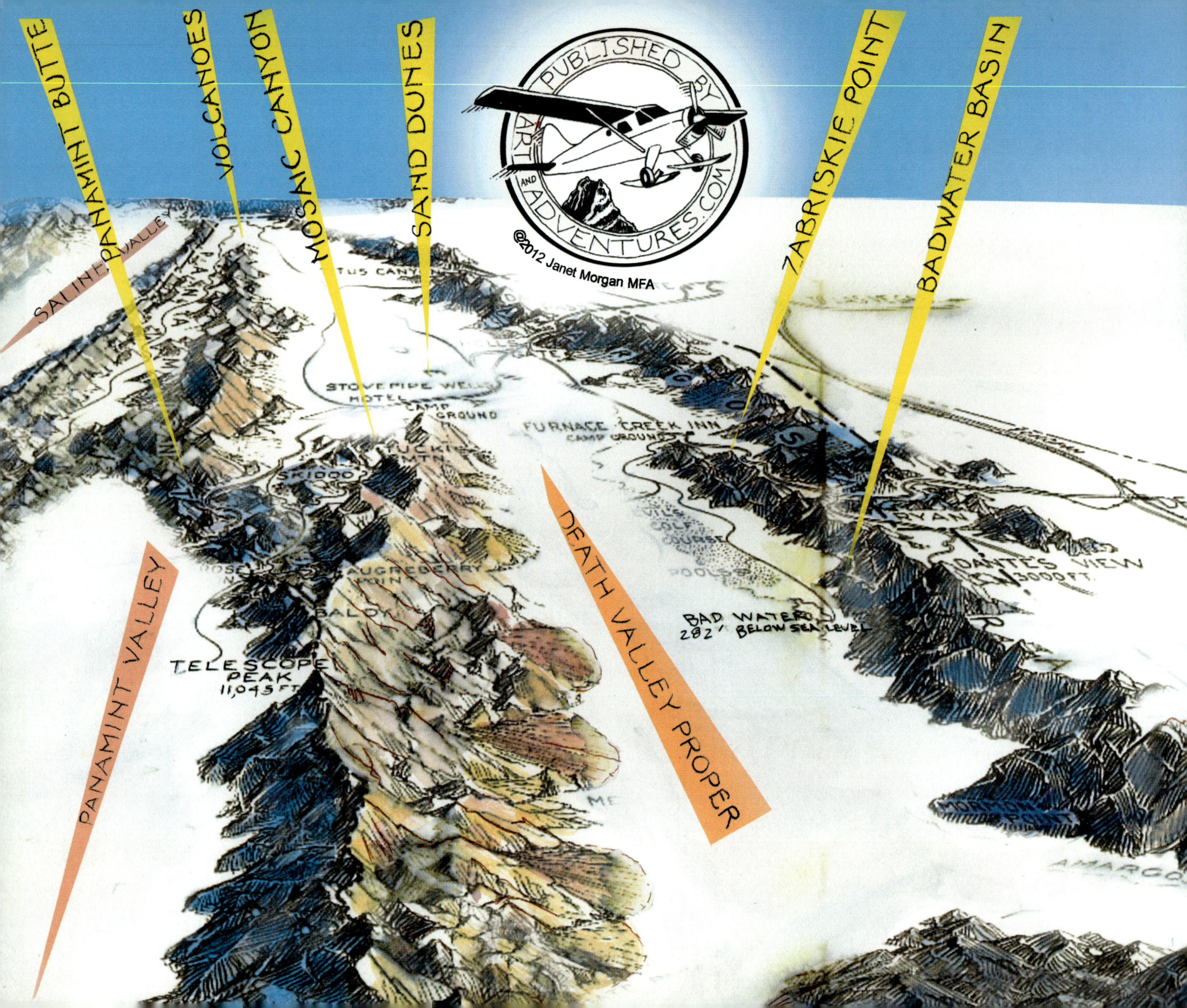
PANAMINT BUTTE
VOLCANOES
MOSAIC CANYON
SAND DUNES
PUBLISHED BY ART AND ADVENTURES.COM
@2012 Janet Morgan MFA
ZABRISKIE POINT
BADWATER BASIN
SALINE VALLEY
STOVEPIPE WELLS HOTEL
CAMP GROUND
FURNACE CREEK INN
CAMP GROUND
TUCKI MTN.
SKIDOO
AUGREBERRY
BALDY
TELESCOPE PEAK 11,045 FT.
PANAMINT VALLEY
DEATH VALLEY PROPER
BAD WATER 282' BELOW SEA LEVEL
DANTES VIEW
RYAN
AMARGO

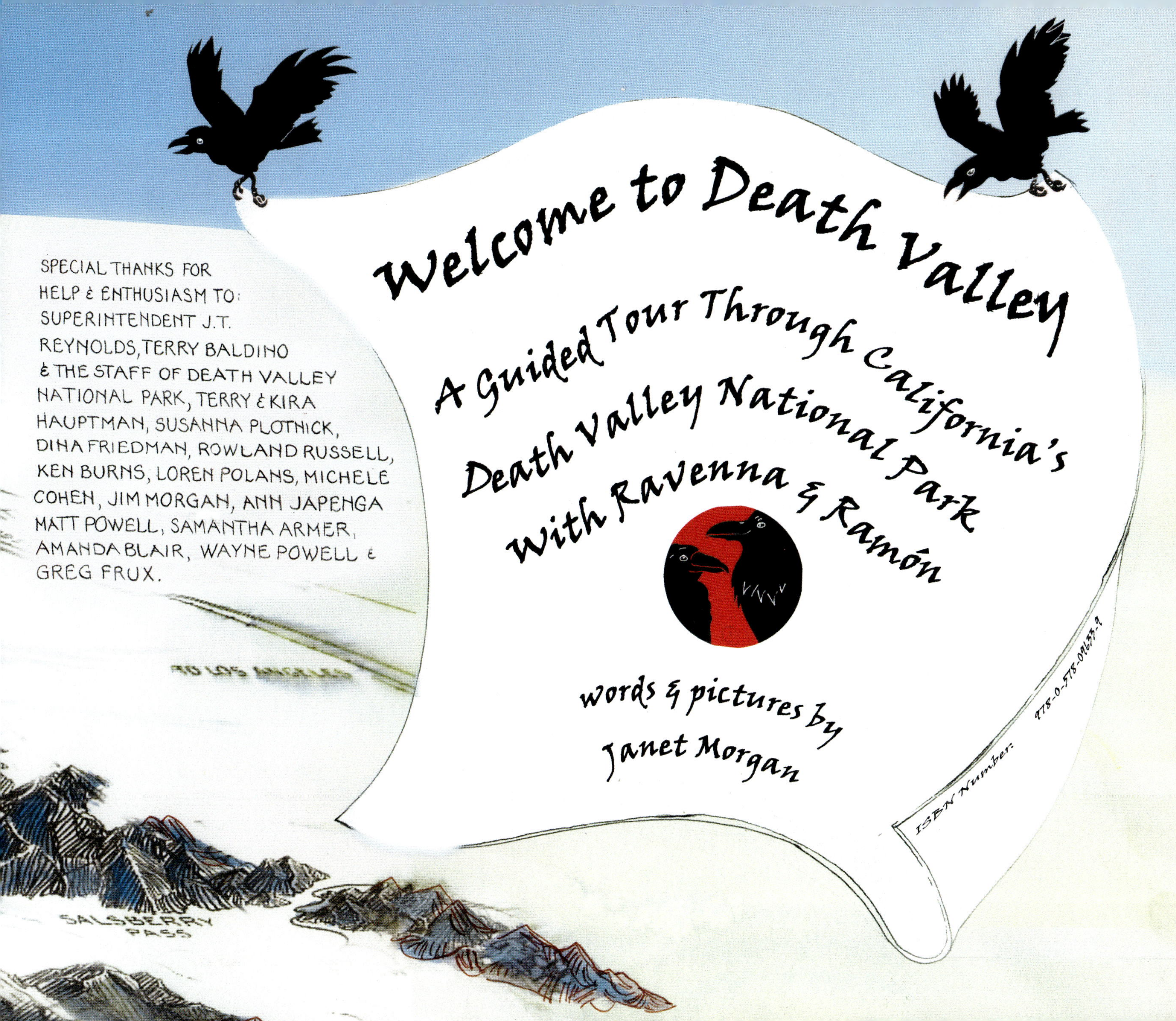
Welcome to Death Valley
A Guided Tour Through California's
Death Valley National Park
With Ravenna & Ramón
words & pictures by
Janet Morgan
ISBN Number. 978-0-578-09633-9
SPECIAL THANKS FOR HELP & ENTHUSIASM TO: SUPERINTENDENT J.T. REYNOLDS, TERRY BALDINO & THE STAFF OF DEATH VALLEY NATIONAL PARK, TERRY & KIRA HAUPTMAN, SUSANNA PLOTNICK, DINA FRIEDMAN, ROWLAND RUSSELL, KEN BURNS, LOREN POLANS, MICHELE COHEN, JIM MORGAN, ANN JAPENGA MATT POWELL, SAMANTHA ARMER, AMANDA BLAIR, WAYNE POWELL & GREG FRUX.
SALSBERRY PASS

Good morning! Welcome to our home.
Let us introduce ourselves...
Our names are Ravenna and Ramón.
We are ravens. We are black like burnt wood.
We gleam and shine in the sun!

We live in Death Valley,
a huge desert that bakes in the summer
and freezes in the winter.
It rains very little and water can be hard to find.
It is a most dangerous place.
But we love it here!

We don't know why you humans call our home Death Valley. For us it is full of life.
Our home has magnificent mountain ranges and curvaceous canyons that slither
on and on and on
and tall tilting sand dunes that slide down into the wide white flats that taste of salt.
And then there are the lizards and insects and dead things to eat! Mmmmm.
We eat just about anything we find so we have plenty of time to play and
explore this magnificent place.

Our friends the Shoshone, who have lived here for many many generations,
love this place as much as we do. They call their home Timbisha - which means rock paint
- it must be that wonderful red ochre mineral that pigments our land.

We love to soar high above our desert home –
to tumble in the air as it runs up the mountainsides,
fleeing the clutch of the hot valley floor.

What is around the corner?

In the Black Mountains we watch the rising sun slowly
pour color over the bones of the earth...
It lights up the great shark's fin of rock they call Manly Beacon –
which rises above the eroded hills of Zabriskie Point.

This is a great place to start our day.

How did this great black river get here?

Around the corner from Manly Beacon we fly over
a swirling blackish river in Gower Gulch.
But wait, it isn't moving! It has stopped in its tracks.

One day not too long ago a storm must have brought enough
water here to make a flood - big enough to carry rocks and mud and earth.
It flowed here and left this dark mysterious river cemented in place.
When this happens they call it a flash flood because it flows very very fast.
The rain that causes the flood can be so far away that you can't see it from here!
So you creatures who cannot fly must always watch the weather reports
when you come to these canyons and gulches.

When we follow this dark river down, it twists and turns
and throws us out into the wide open valley...

We head south to Badwater Basin, named for the springs that taste so bad you wouldn't drink them no matter how thirsty you were.
Badwater is like a huge drained bathtub. It lies at 282 feet below sea level.
If we were at this depth most anywhere else, we would be under the ocean!
It is an enormous playa - a flat area of dried-up lake - made mostly of salt.
It gets very hot here, so it's good to come early in the morning.

This is the lowest and hottest and driest place in North America.
The rain clouds have to climb over four mountain ranges to get here!
People who visit us here love to walk out to the lowest spot,
just so they can say they did it!
We've had our photo taken here many a time by visitors who love
our shiny blackness against the white salt.

Most years Badwater is very dry, one vast expanse of salty nubbly earth. Once in a great while, maybe twice a century, it rains enough to make a lake down here, though it is shallow and salty and not great for swimming. It can be a beautiful bluish green and we have to be careful not to get our feet stuck in the muddy salt at its edge!

Even though it's so hot down here, when you look up at Telescope Peak, you can see snow. When we fly up a mountain here it is like travelling north, like traveling from Florida to Minnesota. The further up you go the cooler and wetter it gets, and in April when it is getting hot in Badwater you need boots with spikes and an ice ax to climb Telescope Peak! Standing in the snow you look back down at the big flat of salt that goes on forever and ever - the playa.
The distance from up there to down here can be measured by stacking 75 Statues of Liberty on top of each other!

Before it gets too hot, let's go to the sand dunes
and see what the creatures of the night have been up to...
Don't run out to the highest dunes just yet - take a look
at the edge of the dunes, where there are bushes and grasses.

Look carefully and you will see the tracks of lizards, birds, beetles, rodents and the wild s-curves of the poisonous sidewinder rattlesnake. By now most of them have found cool places to hide for the day, sleeping until it is dark once again.

Let's fly up over the mountains above Badwater - in a land so arid and parched that it is called the Badlands. The earth is eroded away by wind and water so no life can take hold. But in the rock itself we find rainbows of color - in dusty Desolation Canyon and in the piles of pigment in the Artist's Palette.
Have you ever seen rocks that are mint green and peppermint pink? There are caramel and chocolate rocks too. There is even a mountain called the Chocolate Sundae Mountain!

The sun likes to play with the colors,
adding to them at dawn, washing them out at noon,
filling the shadows with blues of the sky.
The more you watch the colors here the more changes you will see.

In the walls of Bridge Canyon we can hide in tall slots carved by waterfalls. In this land where the rains are rare, how many years did it take to carve these?
It is hard to imagine.
Further up the canyon there is a wall of smooth blue rock that looks like water tumbling down. Often we see humans here talking very excitedly, writing things down and caressing this blue rock. It must have magical powers!

When we fly up and look at the mountains we see that they have skirts flowing down into the valley. These big skirts are called alluvial fans, which mean they are made of alluvium, earth that has been carried downhill by water over many, many years. If you walked from the bottom to the top of one of these skirts, it might take you all day! They are bigger than they look. Sometimes at the top there will be a hidden garden and plants can often be found fringing the bottom edge of the fan where the water stops in its flow.

Here we see the alluvial fans across the valley flowing down toward us. But when we look straight down we see how the fans form circular shapes as they spread out on the flat valley floor.

Looking up from the skirts to the sides of these mountains we often see long horizontal stripes. Many years ago this land was covered with oceans and later with huge lakes. Centuries of minerals and plants and marine animals squished together to become the striped sedimentary layers of these gigantic mountain ranges. These striped mountains are fun to draw – the lines look straight at first but then they wiggle and bend!

Sometimes the earth pitches these striped layers up and sideways, making the mountains look like someone pushed over a layer cake. Earthquakes jar the earth and make the layers slip and slide against each other. Sometimes they look like they are laughing or dancing!
Now let's fly way up over the mountains and see what we can see!

From way up in the sky, we can see the bits of green around the mountains; in the cracks between, in valleys, notches and canyons. Let's glide down there and explore - let's see what we can find.

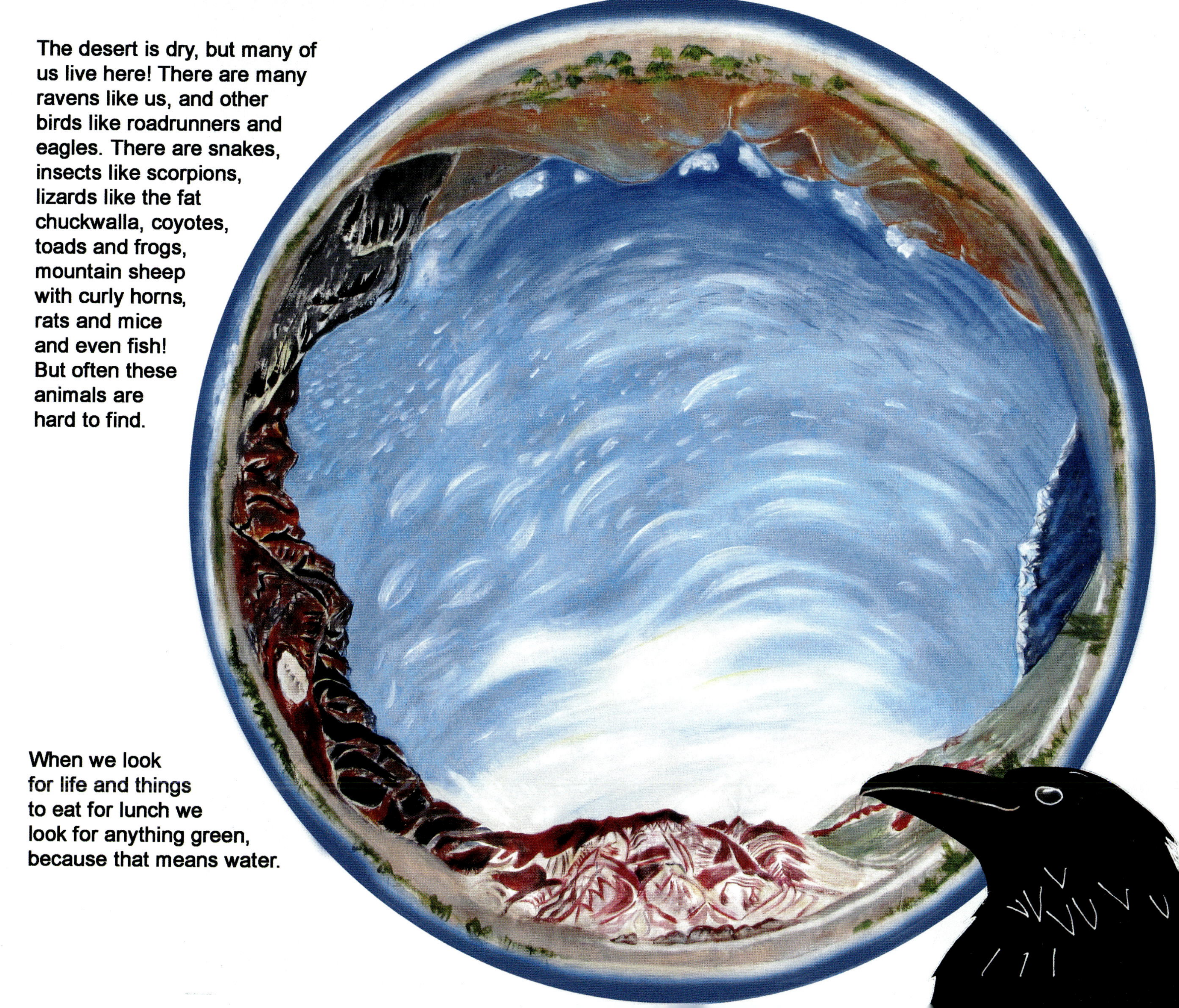

The desert is dry, but many of us live here! There are many ravens like us, and other birds like roadrunners and eagles. There are snakes, insects like scorpions, lizards like the fat chuckwalla, coyotes, toads and frogs, mountain sheep with curly horns, rats and mice and even fish! But often these animals are hard to find.

When we look for life and things to eat for lunch we look for anything green, because that means water.

The narrows of Mosaic Canyon
is carved in a wild dance of tilts and swirls
and hold life only in its wider parts.
The tight places have been scoured down
to slippery rock by the flash floods. Be careful, it is easy to slip here.

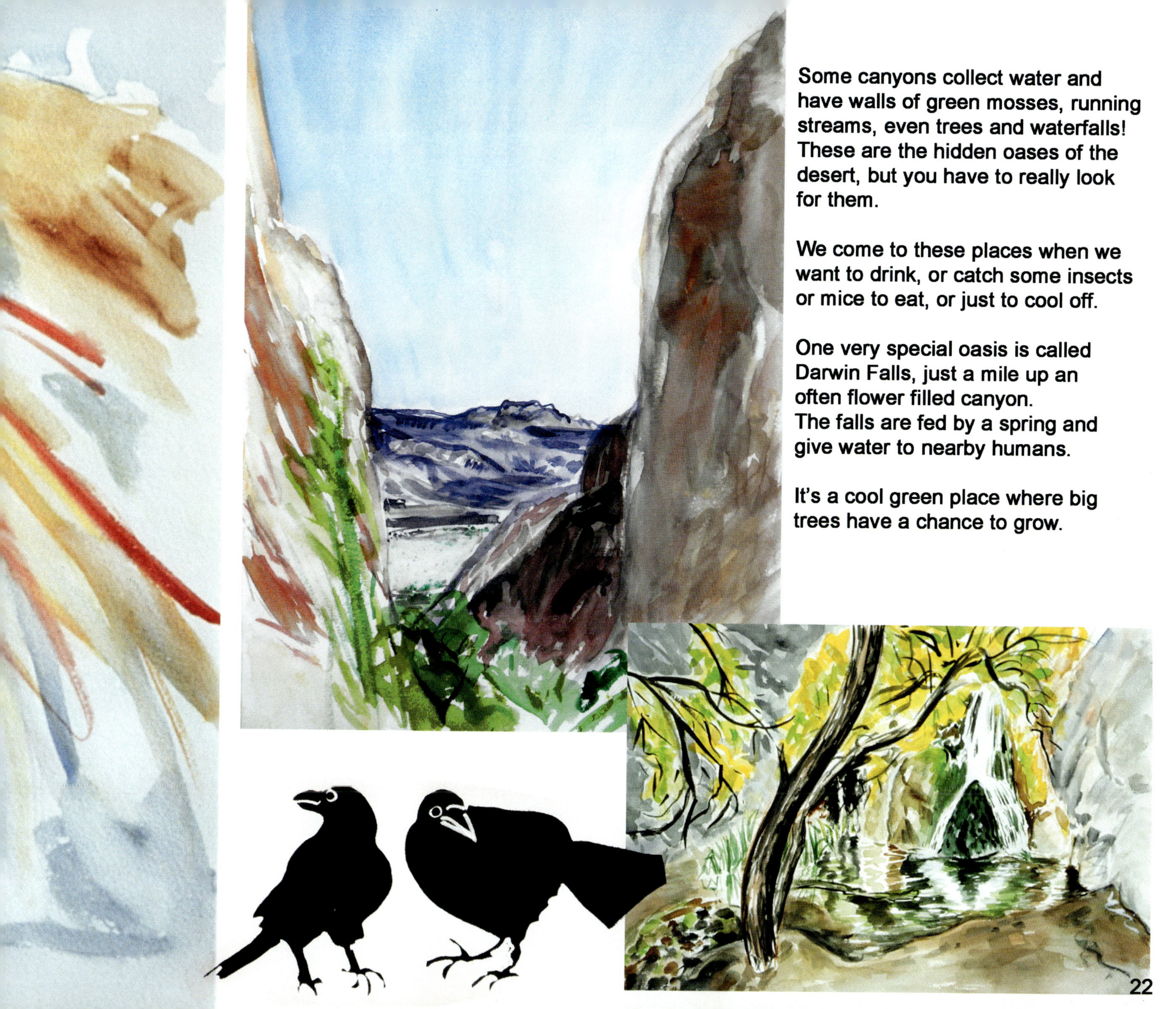

Some canyons collect water and have walls of green mosses, running streams, even trees and waterfalls! These are the hidden oases of the desert, but you have to really look for them.

We come to these places when we want to drink, or catch some insects or mice to eat, or just to cool off.

One very special oasis is called Darwin Falls, just a mile up an often flower filled canyon.
The falls are fed by a spring and give water to nearby humans.

It's a cool green place where big trees have a chance to grow.

The trees that live here in the desert thrive with very little water. Most have small leaves and don't give much shade, like the mesquite tree here on the left.

The tree on the right grows in Surprise Canyon. Surprise Canyon is the only place in the whole park that has running water year round, so some of the trees there are big and green and lush. This big cottonwood gives us lots of shade. It's a nice place to spend the hot part of the day, looking at all the flowers and nibbling on things!

Flowers can bloom all over the park, wherever a little moisture gathers, especially in a wet year. The cactus flowers bloom in bright yellows and vibrant purples.

Flowers here come in all sizes, from the rare yellow Panamint daisy the size of your father's hand, to the tiny belly flowers that you have to lie down on your stomach to see!

We love to take naps here, it's cool and we're surrounded by so many colors.

Let's take a trip way up north to see the giant holes in the ground created by powerful explosions.
These volcanic craters were formed in a few brief moments - many years ago – yet they are young for Death Valley.
The heat and violence of the volcanoes created wildly colored minerals, almost every color you can think of!
At Ubehebe Crater there are lots of oranges and yellows and deep dark blacks.
Not too much grows here. Let's head back south again and look for more colors.

What a lucky day, we're having a late afternoon rain storm!
The colors of the earth and sky have become deep and rich and the smells are all different too.
It feels great after a long hot day.

But sometimes the rain
just stays up in the sky.
You can see it trying
to reach the earth,
but it doesn't hit the ground
– as hard as it tries.

When that happens,
it is called virga.

Our day is almost over. Be sure to watch the colors in the sky as the sun sets. The long slanted shadows show us different shapes as they lie across the valley floor, and the clouds in the sky will put on a show. As the light slowly fades we remember all we have seen; the light on Zabriskie Point, the black still river, the great sand dunes, the striped mountains jumping over themselves, the huge salt playa, and the tracks of the animals who are just now beginning to stir over the sand. We have flown far and our wings are tired!

It is time to say good night!
As the day turns to night and the sun has gone down behind the hills, you might have a full moon like we do tonight. Listen for the coyote's howl.
As many are getting ready to hunt, we ravens are getting ready to sleep. We are joined by our friends from all over who have come to share our roost and tell us what they saw today.
This is our home, Death Valley.
We hope you love it too.